Arthur W. Pink

The Ten Commandments

Baker Books

A Division of Baker Book House Co
Grand Rapids, Michigan 49516

© 1994 by Baker Book House Company

Published by Baker Books
a division of Baker Book House Company
P.O. Box 6287, Grand Rapids, MI 49516-6287

Revised edition published in 1976 by Guardian Press

Printed in the United States of America

ISBN 0-8010-7140-2

CONTENTS

PUBLISHER'S FOREWORD

Today is a day of lawlessness. The spirit of our times is one of unbounded "freedom," one of casting off all restraints, despising all authority. Since God Himself is no longer feared by the majority, many no longer respect the God-ordained authority of governments, parents, church leaders, and educators. Because of abounding iniquity on every hand, the love of many professing Christians for their God and His Law has grown cold, just as Christ prophesied (Matthew 24:12). Yet we see in Holy Scripture that the only *true* freedom is freedom from *sin*. Concerning the purpose of Christ's coming into the world, God's angel Gabriel said to Joseph, "And thou shalt call His name JESUS (that is, 'JEHOVAH is Savior') : for He shall save His people *from* their sins" (Matthew 1:21).

The Lord Jesus said, "Ye shall know the truth, and the truth shall make you free" (John 8:32). Free from what? Free from sin! Jesus Christ Himself *is* the Truth, and to know *Him* is to be free both from the power of reigning sin and from sin's soul-destroying consequences, not simply in the world to come but in this *present* life as well.

The Lord Jesus Himself was well acquainted with the supreme joy of the Godward life of obedience to God's Law and freedom from sin. During His earthly walk, He was a *Lawkeeper* par excellence. To think, that the Second Person of the holy Trinity, Jehovah the eternal Word, the Lawgiver of Israel, was "made of a woman, made under the Law" (Galatians 4:4) for our redemption! Think on this:

5

the salvation that has been *freely given* to you, simply by your having trusted in Christ's blood and righteousness, was procured by Him, your Substitute, at the highest possible cost. The salvation that is "all of grace" to you was *earned*, "all of works," by your Savior! And yet He obeyed every commandment with the purest delight, saying, "My *meat* (food) is to do the will of Him that sent Me, and to finish His work" (John 4:34). Christ could say in the words of Job (23:12), yet with far greater truthfulness, "Neither have I gone back from the commandment of His lips; I have esteemed the words of His mouth more than my necessary food."

Mr. Pink's exposition of God's Moral Law is not *exhaustive*, for that is impossible. The Psalmist says, "I have seen the end of all perfection: but Thy commandment is exceeding broad" (Psalm 119:96). Nevertheless, Mr. Pink gets to the root of man's need. He ably demonstrates the way in which God's Spirit uses the Law: (1) in bringing men to a saving knowledge of Jesus Christ (by bringing them to the end of themselves); and (2) in producing in them an increasing "family resemblance," a holy likeness to their Father in heaven (which is the fruit of true saving faith).

If you will read this book prayerfully, then God will graciously enable you to cry out with the Psalmist, "O how love I Thy law! It is my meditation all the day" (Psalm 119:97).

INTRODUCTORY CONSIDERATIONS

There are two things which are indispensable to the Christian's life: first, a clear knowledge of duty, and second, a conscientious practice of duty corresponding to his knowledge. As we can have no well-grounded hope of eternal salvation without obedience, so we can have no sure rule of obedience without knowledge. Although there may be knowledge without practice, yet there cannot possibly be practice of God's will without knowledge. And therefore that we might be informed what we ought to do and what to avoid, it has pleased the Ruler and Judge of all the earth to prescribe for us laws for the regulating of our actions. When we had miserably defaced the Law of nature originally written in our hearts, so that many of its commandments were no longer legible, it seemed good to the Lord to transcribe that Law into the Scriptures, and in the Ten Commandments we have a summary of the same.

First let us consider *their promulgation.* The manner in which the Decalogue was formally delivered to Israel was very awe-inspiring, yet replete with valuable instruction for us. First, the people were commanded to spend two days in preparing themselves, by a ceremonial cleansing from all external pollution, before they were ready to stand in the presence of God (Ex. 19:10, 11). This teaches us that serious preparation of heart and mind must be made before we come to wait before God in His ordinances and receive a word at His mouth; and that if Israel must sanctify themselves in order to appear before God at Sinai, how much more must we sanctify ourselves that we may be meet to appear before God in Heaven. Next, the mount on which God appeared was to be fenced, with a strict prohibition that none should presume to approach the holy mount (19: 12, 13). This teaches us that God is infinitely superior to us and due our utmost reverence, and intimates the strictness of His Law.

Next we have a description of the fearful manifestation in which Jehovah appeared to deliver His Law (Ex. 19: 18, 19), which was designed to affect the people of Israel with an awe for His authority and to signify that if God were so terrible in the giving of the Law, when He comes to judge us for its violation how much more so will He be? When God had delivered the Ten Words, so greatly affected were the people that they entreated Moses to act as a mediator and interpreter between God and them (20:18, 19). This teaches us that when the Law is delivered to us directly by God it is (in itself) the ministration of condemnation and death, but as it is delivered to us by the Mediator, Christ, we may hear and observe it (see Gal. 3:19; I Cor. 9:21; Gal. 6:2). Accordingly Moses went up into the mount and received the Law, inscribed by God's own finger upon two tables of stone, signifying that our hearts are naturally so hard that none but the finger of God can make any impression of His Law upon them. Those tables were broken by Moses in his holy zeal (Ex. 32:19), and God wrote them a second time (34:1). This signifies that the Law of Nature was written on our hearts at creation, broken when we fell in Adam, and rewritten in our hearts at regeneration (Heb. 10:16).

But some may ask, "Has not the Law been fully abrogated by the coming of Christ into the world? Would you bring us under that heavy yoke of bondage which none has ever been able to bear? Does not the New Testament expressly declare that we are not under the Law, but under Grace; that Christ was made under the Law to free His people therefrom? Is not an attempt to overawe men's conscience by the authority of the Decalogue a legalistic imposition, altogether at variance with that Christian liberty which the Savior has brought in by His obedience unto death?" We answer thus: So far from the Law being abolished by the coming of Christ into this world, He Himself emphatically stated, "Think not that I am come to destroy the Law or the Prophets (the enforcers thereof): I am come not to destroy, but to fulfill. For verily I say unto you, Till heaven and earth pass, one jot or one tittle shall in nowise pass from the law, till all be fulfilled" (Matt. 5:17, 18). True, the Christian is not under the Law as a Covenant of Works nor as a ministration of condemnation, but he *is* under it as a rule of life and a means of sanctification.

Second, let us consider *their uniqueness*. This appears first in that this revelation of God at Sinai, which was to serve for all coming ages as the grand expression of His holiness and the summation of man's duty, was attended with such awe-inspiring phenomena that the very manner of their publication plainly showed that God Himself assigned to the Decalogue peculiar importance. The Ten Commandments were uttered by God in an audible voice, with the fearful adjuncts of clouds and darkness, thunders and lightnings and the sound of a trumpet, and they were the only parts of Divine Revelation so spoken—none of the ceremonial or civil precepts were thus distinguished. Those Ten Words, and they alone, were written by the finger of God upon tables of stone, and they alone were deposited in the holy ark for safekeeping. Thus, in the unique honor conferred upon the Decalogue, we may perceive its paramount importance in the divine government.

Third, let us consider *their springs,* which is love. Far too little emphasis has been placed upon their Divine preface: "And God spake all these words, saying, I am the Lord thy God, which have brought thee out of the land of Egypt, out of the house of bondage." Whatever of awful grandeur and solemn majesty attended the promulgation of the Law, nevertheless, it had its foundation *in love.* The Law proceeded from God as a clear expression of His character as both the gracious Redeemer and righteous Lord of His people. The obvious conclusion and all-important principle that must be drawn from this understanding is this: redemption necessitates conformity to God's character and order in those who are redeemed. Not only was God's giving of the Decalogue an act of love, but love was the basis upon which it was received by His people, for only thus could there be a conformity, an essential likeness, between a redeeming God and a redeemed people. The words at the close of the second commandment, "showing mercy unto thousands of them *that love Me* and keep My commandments," make it crystal clear that the only obedience which God accepts is that which proceeds from an affectionate heart. The Savior declared that the requirements of the Law were all summed up in loving God with all our hearts and loving our neighbors as ourselves.

Fourth, let us consider *their perpetuity.* That the Decalogue is binding upon every man in each succeeding generation is evident from many considerations. First, as the necessary and unchanging expression of God's rectitude, its authority over all moral agents becomes inevitable: the character of God Himself must change before the Law (the rule of His government) can be revoked.

This is the Law that was given to man at his creation from which his subsequent apostasy could not relieve him. The Moral Law is founded on relations which subsist wherever there are creatures endowed with reason and volition. Second, Christ Himself rendered to the Law a perfect obedience, thereby leaving us an example, that we should follow in His steps. Third, the Apostle to the Gentiles specifically raised the question "Do we then make void the Law through faith?" and answered, "God forbid: yea, we establish the Law" (Rom. 3:31). Finally, the perpetuity of the Law appears in God's writing it in the hearts of His people at their new birth (Jer. 31:33; Ezek. 36:26, 27).

Fifth, we pass on to say a word upon *the number* of the commandments of the Moral Law, ten being indicative of their completeness. This is emphasized in Scripture by their being expressly designated "the Ten Words" (Ex. 34:28 margin), which intimates that they formed by themselves an entire whole made up of the necessary, and no more than the necessary, complement of its parts. It was on account of this symbolic import of the number that the plagues upon Egypt were precisely that many, forming as such a complete round of Divine judgments. And it was for the same reason that the transgressions of the Hebrews in the wilderness were allowed to proceed till the same number had been reached: when they had "sinned these ten times" (Num. 14:21) they had "filled up the measure of their iniquities." Hence also the consecration of the tithes or tenths: the whole increase was represented by ten, and one of these was set apart for the Lord in token of *all* being derived from Him and held for Him.

Sixth, we consider *their division*. As God never acts without good reason we may be sure He had some particular design in writing the Law upon two tables. This design is evident on the surface, for the very substance of these precepts, which together comprehend the sum of righteousness, separates them into two distinct groups, the first respecting our obligations Godward, and the second our obligations manward, the former treating of what belongs peculiarly to the worship of God, the latter of the duties of charity in our social relations. Utterly worthless is that righteousness which abstains from acts of violence against our fellows while we withhold from the Majesty of heaven the glory which is His due. Equally vain is it to pretend to be worshippers of God if we refuse those offices of love which are due to our neighbors. Abstaining from fornication is more than neutralized if I blasphemously take the Lord's name in vain, while the most punctilious worship is rejected by Him while I steal or lie.

Nor do the duties of Divine worship fill up the first table because they are, as Calvin terms them, "the head of religion," but as he rightly adds, they are "the very soul of it, constituting all its life and vigor," for without the fear of God, men preserve no equity and love among themselves. If the principle of piety be lacking, whatever justice, mercy, and temperance men may practice among themselves, it is vain in the sight of Heaven; whereas if God be accorded His rightful place in our hearts and lives, venerating Him as the Arbiter of right and wrong, this will constrain us to deal equitably with our fellows. Opinion has varied as to how the Ten Words were divided, as to whether the fifth ended the first table or began the second. Personally, we incline decidedly to the former: because parents stand to us in the place of God while we are young; because in Scripture parents are never regarded as "neighbors"—on an equality; and because each of the first five commandments contain the phrase "the Lord thy God," which is not found in any of the remaining five.

Seventh, let us consider *their spirituality.* "The Law is spiritual" (Rom. 7:14), not only because it proceeds from a spiritual Legislator, but because it demands something more than the mere obedience of external conduct, namely, the internal obedience of the heart to its uttermost extent. It is only as we perceive that the Decalogue extends to thoughts and desires of the heart that we discover how much there is in ourselves in direct opposition to it. God requires *truth* "in the inward parts" (Psa. 51:6) and prohibits the smallest deviation from holiness even in our imaginations. The fact that the Law takes cognizance of our most secret dispositions and intentions, that it demands the holy regulation of our mind, affections, and will, and that it requires all our obedience to proceed from love at once demonstrates its Divine origin. No other law ever professed to govern the *spirit* of man, but He who searches the heart claims nothing less. This high spirituality of the Law was evidenced by Christ when He insisted that an unchaste look was adultery and that malignant anger was a breach of the sixth commandment.

Eighth, we consider *their office.* The first use of the Moral Law is to reveal the only righteousness which is acceptable to God, and at the same time to discover to us our own unrighteousness. Sin has blinded our judgment, filled us with self-love, and wrought in us a false sense of our own sufficiency. But if we seriously compare ourselves with the high and holy demands of God's Law, we are made aware of our groundless insolence, convicted of our pollution and guilt, and made conscious of our lack of strength to do what is required of us. Calvin, in his *Institutes of the Christian Religion* (Book II, Chapter 7, section 7), says, "Thus the Law is a kind of mirror. As in a mirror we discover any stains upon our face, so in the Law we behold, first, our impotence; then, in consequence of it, our iniquity; and, finally, the curse, as the consequence of both." Its second use is to restrain the wicked, who though they have no concern for God's glory and no thought of pleasing Him, yet refrain from many outward acts of sin through fear of its terrible penalty. Though this commends them not to God, it is a benefit to the community in which they live. Third, the law is the believer's rule of life, to direct him, and to keep him dependent upon Divine grace.

Ninth, we consider *its sanctions.* Not only has the Lord brought us under infinite obligations for having redeemed us from sin's slavery, not only has He given His people such a sight and sense of His awe-inspiring majesty as to beget in them a reverence for His sovereignty, but He has been pleased to provide additional inducements for us to yield to His authority, gladly perform His bidding, and shrink with abhorrence from what He forbids, by subjoining promises and threatenings, saying, "For I the Lord thy God am a jealous God, visiting the iniquity of the fathers upon the children unto the third and fourth generation of them that hate Me; and showing mercy unto thousands of them that love Me, and keep My commandments." Thus we are informed that those who perform His bidding shall not labor in vain, just as rebels shall not escape with impunity.

And *tenth and finally,* we consider *their interpretation.* "Thy commandment" said the Psalmist "is exceeding broad" (119:96). So comprehensive is the Moral Law that its authority extends to all the moral actions of our lives. The rest of the Scriptures are but a commentary on the Ten Commandments, either exciting us to obedience by arguments, alluring us by promises, restraining from transgressions by threatenings, or spurring us to the one and withholding us from the other by examples recorded in the historical portions. Rightly understood the precepts of the New Testament are but explications, amplifications, and applications of the Ten Commandments. It should be carefully observed that in the things expressly commanded or forbidden there is always implied more than is formally stated. But let us be more specific. *First,* in each Commandment the chief duty or sin is taken as representative of all the lesser duties or sins, and the overt act is taken as representative of all related affections. Whatever specific sin be named, all the sins of the same kind, with all the causes and provocations thereof, are forbidden, for Christ expounded the sixth commandment as condemning not only actual murder, but also rash anger in the heart. *Second,* when any vice is forbidden, the contrary virtue is enjoined, and when any virtue is commanded, the contrary vice is condemned. For example, in the third God forbids the taking of His name in vain, so by necessary consequence the hallowing of His name is commanded. And as the eighth forbids stealing, so it requires the contrary duty—earning our living and paying for what we receive (Eph. 4:28).

THE FIRST COMMANDMENT

"And God spake all these words, saying, I am the Lord thy God, which have brought thee out of the land of Egypt, out of the house of bondage" (Ex. 20:1, 2). This Preface to the Moral Law is to be regarded as having equal respect to *all* the Ten Commandments (and not to the first one only), containing as it does the most weighty arguments to enforce our obedience to them. As it is the custom of kings and governors to prefix their names and titles before the edicts set forth by them, to obtain the more attention and veneration to what they publish, so with the great God, the King of kings, being about to proclaim a Law for His subjects, that He might affect them with a deeper reverence for His authority and make them the more afraid to transgress those statutes which are enacted by so mighty a Potentate and so glorious a Majesty, blazons His august Name upon them.

What has just been pointed out above is clearly established by those awe-inspiring words of Moses to Israel: "That thou mayest fear this glorious and fearful name, THE LORD THY GOD" (Deut. 28:58). "I am the Lord thy God." The word for "Lord" is "Jehovah," who is the Supreme, Eternal and Self-existent One, the force of which is (as it were) spelled out for us in "which was, and is, and is to come" (Rev. 4:8). The word for "God" is "Elohim," the plural of Eloah, for though He be one in nature yet is He three in His Persons. And this Jehovah, the Supreme Object of worship, is "thy GOD," because in

16

the past He was thy Creator, in the present He is thy Ruler, and in the future He will be thy Judge. In addition, He is the "God" of His elect by covenant relationship and therefore their Redeemer. Thus, our obedience to His Law is enforced by these considerations: His absolute authority, to beget fear in us—He is "the Lord thy God"; His benefits and mercies, to engage love—"which brought thee out of the (antitypical) house of bondage."

"Thou shalt have no other gods before Me" (Ex. 20:3) is the first Commandment. Let us briefly consider its meaning. We note its singular number: "thou" not "ye," addressed to each person separately, because each of us is concerned therein. "Thou shalt *have* no other gods" has the force of, thou shalt own, possess, seek, desire, love or worship none other. No "other *gods*"; they are called such not because they are so, either by nature or by office (Psa. 82:6), but because the corrupt hearts of men make and esteem them such—as in "whose god is their belly" (Phil. 3:19). "Before Me" or "My face," the force of which is best ascertained by His word to Abraham, "Walk before Me and be thou perfect" or "upright" (Gen. 17:1) —conduct thyself in the realization that thou are ever in My presence, that Mine eye is continually upon thee. This is very searching. We are so apt to rest contented if we can but approve ourselves before men and maintain a fair show of godliness outwardly; but Jehovah searches our innermost being and we cannot conceal from Him any secret lust or hidden idol.

Let us next consider the positive duty enjoined by this first Commandment. Briefly stated it is this: thou shalt choose, worship and serve Jehovah as thy God, and Him only. Being who He is—thy Maker and Ruler, the Sum of all excellency, the supreme Object of worship—He admits of no rival and none can vie with Him. See then the absolute reasonableness of this demand and the madness of contravening it. This commandment requires from us a disposition and conduct suited to the relation in which we stand to the Lord as our God, who is the only adequate Object of our love and the only One able to satisfy the soul. It requires that we have a love for Him stronger than all other affections, that we take Him for our highest portion, that we serve and obey Him supremely. It requires that all those services and acts of worship which we render unto the true God be made with the utmost sincerity and devotion (implied in the "before Me"), excluding negligence on the one hand and hypocrisy on the other.

In pointing out the *duties* required by this Commandment we cannot do better than to quote the Westminster Confession of Faith. They are "the knowing and acknowledging of God to be the only true God, and our God (I Chron. 28:9; Deut. 26:17, etc.) ; and to worship and glorify Him accordingly (Psa. 95:6, 7; Matt. 4:10, etc.), by thinking (Mal. 3:16), meditating (Psa. 63:6), remembering (Eccl. 12:1), highly esteeming (Psa. 71:19), honouring (Mal. 1:6), adoring (Isa. 45:23), choosing (Josh. 24:15), loving (Deut. 6:5), desiring (Psa. 73:25), fearing of Him (Isa. 8:13), believing Him (Ex. 14:31), trusting (Isa. 26:4), hoping (Psa. 103:7), delighting (Psa. 37:4), rejoicing in Him (Psa. 32:11), being zealous for Him (Rom. 12:11), calling upon him, giving all praise and thanks (Phil. 4:6), and yielding all obedience and submission to Him with the whole man (Jer. 7:23), being careful in all things to please Him (I John 3:22), and sorrowful when in anything he is offended (Jer. 31:18; Psa. 119:136), and walking humbly with Him (Micah 6:8)."

Those duties may be summarized in these chief ones. First, the diligent and lifelong seeking after a fuller knowledge of God as He is revealed in His Word and works, for we cannot worship an unknown God. Second, the loving of God with all our faculties and strength, which consists of an earnest panting after Him, and deep joy in Him, and a holy zeal for Him. Third, the fearing of God, which consists of an awe of his majesty, supreme reverence for His authority, and a desire for His glory: as the love of God is the motive-spring of obedience, so the fear of God is the great deterrent of disobedience. Fourth, the worshipping of God according to His appointments, the principal aids to which are these: study of and meditation upon the Word, prayer, and putting into practice what we are taught.

"Thou shalt have no other Gods before Me." That is, thou shalt not give unto anyone or anything in Heaven or on earth that inward heart affiance, loving veneration, and dependence that is due only to the true God; thou shalt not transfer to another that which belongs alone unto Him. Nor must we attempt to divide them between God and another, for no man can serve two masters. The great *sins forbidden* by this Commandment are these: first willful ignorance of God and His will through despising those means by which we may acquaint ourselves with Him; second, atheism or the denial of God; third, idolatry or the setting up of false and fictitious gods; fourth, disobedience and self-will or the open defiance of God; and fifth, all inordinate and immoderate affections or the setting of our hearts and minds upon other objects.

They are idolaters and transgressors of this first commandment who manufacture a "God" as a figment of their own minds. Such are the Unitarians, who deny that there are three Persons in the Godhead. Such are Romanists, who supplicate the Savior's mother and affirm that the pope has power to forgive sins. Such are the vast majority of Arminians, who believe in a disappointed and defeated Deity. Such are sensual epicureans (Phil. 3:19), for there are inward idols as well as external. "These men have set up their idols in their hearts" (Ezek. 14:3). The Apostle Paul speaks of "covetousness which *is* idolatry"

(Col. 3:5) and, by impartial reasoning, so are *all* immoderate desires. That object to which we render those desires and services which are due alone to the Lord is our "God," whether it be self, gold, fame, pleasure, or friends. What is your God? To what is your life devoted?

THE SECOND COMMANDMENT

"Thou shalt not make unto thee any graven image or any likeness of any thing that is in heaven above, or that is in the earth beneath, or that is in the water under the earth: thou shalt not bow down thyself to them, nor serve them: for I the Lord thy God am a jealous God, visiting the iniquity of the fathers upon the children unto the third and fourth generation of them that hate Me, and showing mercy unto thousands of them that love Me and keep My commandments" (Ex. 20:4-6). Though this second Commandment is closely related to the first, yet there is a clear distinction between them, which may be expressed in a variety of ways. As the first Commandment concerns the choice of the true God as our God, so the second tells of our actual profession of His worship; as the former fixes the Object so this fixes the mode of religious worship. As in the first commandment Jehovah had proclaimed Himself to be the true God, so here He reveals His nature and how He is to be honored.

"Thou shalt not make unto thee any graven image . . . thou shalt not bow down thyself to them." This commandment strikes against a desire, or should we say a disease, which is deeply rooted in the human heart, namely, to bring in some aids to the worship of God, beyond those which He has appointed—material aids, things which can be perceived by the senses. Nor is the reason for this difficult to find: God is incorporeal, invisible, and can be realized only by a *spiritual* principle, and since that principle

21

is dead in fallen man, he naturally seeks that which accords with his carnality. But how different is it with those who have been quickened by the Holy Spirit. No one who truly knows God as a living reality needs any images to aid his devotions; none who enjoys daily communion with Christ requires any pictures of Him to help him to pray and adore, for he conceives of Him by faith and not by fancy.

"Thou shalt not make unto thee any graven image or any likeness." It is a manifest straining of this precept to make it condemn all statuary and paintings: it is not the ingenuity of making but the stupidity in the worshipping of them which is condemned, as is clear from the words "thou shalt not bow down thyself to them," and from the fact that God Himself shortly afterwards ordered Israel to "make two cherubim of gold of beaten work" for the mercy seat (Ex. 25:18) and later the serpent of brass. Since God is a spiritual, invisible, and omnipotent Being, to represent Him as being of a material and limited form is a falsehood and an insult to His majesty. Under this most extreme corruption of mode—image worship—all erroneous modes of Divine homage are here forbidden. The legitimate worship of God must not be profaned by any superstitious rites.

This second Commandment is but the negative way of saying "God is Spirit: and they that worship Him must worship Him in spirit and in truth" (John 4:24). If it be asked, what are *the duties here required?* The answer is this: "The receiving, observing, and keeping pure and entire, all such religious worship and ordinances as God has instituted in His Word (Deut. 32:46, 47; Matt. 28:20; Acts 2:42; I Tim 6:13, 14); particularly prayer and thanksgiving in the name of Christ (Phil. 4:6, Eph. 5:20); the reading, preaching, and hearing of the Word (Deut. 17:18, 19; Acts 15:21; II Tim. 4:2, etc.); the administration and receiving of the sacraments (Matt. 28:19; I Cor. 11:21-30);

church government and discipline (Matt. 18:15, 17; 16:19; I Cor. 5) ; the ministry and maintenance thereof (Eph. 4:11, 12, etc.) ; religious fasting (I Cor. 8:5) ; swearing by the name of God (Deut. 6:13) , and vowing unto Him (Isa. 19:21; Psa. 76:11) ; as also the disapproving, detesting, opposing, all false worship (Acts 16:16, 17, etc.) ; and according to each one's place and calling, removing it, and all monuments of idolatry (Deut. 7:5; Isa. 30:22) "—Westminster Confession of Faith. To this we would simply add, there is required of us a diligent preparation before we enter upon any holy exercise (Eccl. 5:1) and a right disposition of mind in the act itself. For example, we must not hear or read the Word just to satisfy curiosity, but that we may learn how better to please God.

In the forbidding of images God by parity of reason prohibits *all* other modes and means of worship not appointed by Him. Every form of worship, even of the true God Himself, which is contrary to or diverse from what the Lord has prescribed in His Word, and which is called by the apostle "will worship" (Col. 2:23) , together with all corruptions of the true worship of God and all inclinations of heart toward superstition in the service of God are reprehended by this Comandment. No scope whatever is here permitted to the inventive faculty of man. Christ condemned the religious washing of the hands, because it was a human addition to the Divine regulations. In like manner this Commandment denounces the modern passion for ritualism (the dressing up of simplicity in Divine worship) , as also the magical virtues ascribed to, or even the special influences of, the Lord's Supper, still more so the use of a crucifix. So also it condemns a neglect of God's worship, the leaving undone the service which God has commanded.

The Scriptures have set us bounds for worship, to which we must not add, and from which we must not diminish. In the application of this principle we need to distinguish sharply between the substantials and the incidentals of worship. Anything which men seek to impose upon us as a part of Divine worship, if it be not expressly required of us in the Scriptures—such as bowing the knee at the name of Jesus, crossing ourselves, etc.—is to be abominated. But if certain circumstantials and modifications of worship are practiced by those with whom we meet, even though there be no express Scripture for them, they are to be submitted unto by us, providing they are such things as tend to decency and order and distract not from the solemnity and devotion of spiritual worship. That was a wise rule inculcated by Ambrose: "If thou will neither give offense nor take offense, conform thyself to all the lawful customs of the churches where thou comest." It is a grievous breaking of this commandment if we neglect any of the ordinances of worship which God has appointed. So too if we engage in the same hypocritically, with coldness of affection, wanderings of mind, lack of holy zeal, or in unbelief, honoring God with our lips while our hearts are far from Him.

This Commandment is enforced by three reasons. The *first* is drawn from the Person who pronounces judgment upon those who break it. He is described by His relationship, "thy God"; by the might of His power, for the Hebrew word for "God" here is "the Strong One", able to vindicate His honor and avenge all insults thereto; and by a similitude taken from the state of wedlock, wherein unfaithfulness results in summary punishment—He is a "jealous God." It is the Lord speaking after the manner of men, intimating that He will not spare those who mock Him. "They provoked Him to jealousy with strange gods, with abominations provoked they Him to anger. . . . They have moved Me to jealousy with that which is not God" (Deut. 32:16-21 ff) .

Secondly, a sore judgment is threatened: "visiting the iniquity of the fathers upon the children unto the third and fourth generation of them that hate Me." "Visiting" is a figurative expression, which signifies that after a space of time, in which God appears to have taken no notice or to have forgotten, He then shows by His providences that He *has* observed the evil ways and doings of men. "Shall I not visit for these things? saith the Lord: and shall not My soul be avenged on such a nation as this?" (Jer. 5:9, and cf. 32:18; Matt. 23:34-36). This was designed to deter men from idolatry by an appeal to their natural affections. "The curse of the Lord righteously rests not only on the person of an impious man, but also on the whole of his family" (John Calvin). It is a terrible thing to pass on to children a false conception of God, either by precept or by example. The penalty inflicted corresponds to the crime: it is not only that God punishes the child for the offenses committed by the parents, but that He gives them over unto the same transgressions and then deals with them accordingly, for the example of parents is not sufficient warrant for us to commit sin.

Thirdly, there is a most blessed encouragement to obedience, in the form of a gracious promise: "Showing mercy unto thousands of them that love Me, and keep My commandments." To the same effect He assures us, "The just man walketh in his integrity: his children are blessed after him" (Prov. 20:7). Love for God is evidenced by a keeping of His commandments. Papists contend that their use of images is with the object of promoting love, by keeping a visible image before them as an aid; but God says it is because they *hate* Him. This promise to show mercy unto thousands of the descendants of those who truly love God does not express a universal principle, as is clear from the cases of Isaac having a godless Esau and David an Absalom. "The Legislator never intended to establish in this case such an invariable rule as would derogate from His own free choice . . . When the Lord exhibits one example of this blessing, He affords a proof of

His constant and perpetual favor to His worshippers"
(Calvin). Observe that here, as elsewhere in Scripture
(Jude 14, for example), God speaks of "thousands" (*and
not* "millions," as men so often do) of them that love Him
and who manifest the genuineness of their love by keeping His commandments. His flock is but a "little" one
(Luke 12:32). What cause for thanksgiving unto God have
those who are born of pious parents, whose parents
treasure up not wrath for them, but prayers!

THE THIRD COMMANDMENT

"Thou shalt not take the name of the Lord thy God in vain: for the Lord will not hold him guiltless that taketh His name in vain" (Ex. 20:7). As the second commandment concerns the manner in which God is to be worshipped (namely, according to His revealed will), so this one bids us worship Him with that frame of spirit which is agreeable to the dignity and solemnity of such an exercise and the majesty of Him with whom we have to do: that is, with the utmost sincerity, humility, and reverence. *"Fear* this glorious and fearful name, THE LORD THY GOD" (Deut. 28:58). O what high thoughts we ought to entertain of such a Being! In what holy awe should we stand of Him! "The end of this Precept is that the Lord will have the majesty of His name to be held inviolably sacred by us. Whatever we think and whatever we say of Him should savor of His excellency, correspond to the sacred sublimity of His name, and tend to the exaltation of His magnificence" (Calvin). Anything pertaining to God should be spoken of with the greatest sobriety.

Let us first endeavor to point out *the scope* and comprehensiveness of this commandment. By the Name of the Lord our God is signified God Himself as He is made known to us, including everything through which He has been pleased to reveal Himself: His Word, His titles, His attributes, His ordinances, His works. The Name of God stands for His very nature and being, as in Psa. 20:1; 135:3; John 1:12, etc. Sometimes the name of God is taken for the entire system of Divine Truth: "we will walk in the Name of the Lord our God" (Micah 4:5) —in that way of Truth and worship which He has appointed. "I have manifested Thy Name unto the men Thou gavest Me" (John 17:6) : that is, Christ instructed them in the Heavenly doctrine. But usually, and more specifically, the Name of God refers to that by which He is called and made known to us. To *take* His Name" means to employ or make use of the same, as the Object of our thoughts or the Subject of our speech. Not to take His Name "in vain" is the negative way of saying it must be held in the utmost awe and used holily in thought and word and deed.

It will thus be seen that this Commandment requires us *to* make mention of the Name of God. Since He has given us so many and gracious discoveries of Himself, it would evince the vilest contempt of the greatest of privileges if we expressed no regard to those discoveries and made no use of the same. Those who make no religious profession, and desire not to be instructed in those things which relate to the Divine glory, are guilty of thus slighting the Most High. But we make use of God's Name in public worship, in private prayer, and when taking religious oaths or making solemn vows. When we draw nigh to God in prayer we should adore the Divine perfections with a becoming humility, as did Abraham (Gen. 18:27), Jacob (Gen. 32:10), Moses (Ex. 15:11), Solomon (I Kings 8:33), Hezekiah (II Kings 19:15), Daniel (9:4), and as the inhabitants of Heaven do (Rev. 4:10, 11). Negatively, this Commandment prohibits all dishonoring thoughts of God, all needless, flippant, profane, or blasphemous mention of Him, any irreverent use of His Word, any murmurings against His providence, any abuse of anything by which He has made Himself known.

Let us now point out more specifically some of the ways in which God's name may be taken in vain. The first is, when it is used without propounding to ourselves a proper end. And there are but two ends which can warrant our use of any of His names, titles, or attributes: for His glory and for the edification of ourselves and others. Whatever is besides these is frivolous and evil, affording no sufficient ground for us to make mention of such a great and holy Name, which is so full of glory and majesty. Unless our speech is designedly directed to the advancement of the Divine glory or the promotion of the benefit of those to whom we speak, we are not justified in having God's ineffable Name upon our lips. He accounts Himself highly insulted when we mention His name to idle purpose.

God's Name is taken in vain by us when we use it without due consideration and reverence. Whenever we make mention of Him before whom the seraphim veil their faces, we ought seriously and solemnly to ponder His infinite majesty and glory, and bow our hearts in deepest prostration before that Name. How can they, who think and speak of the great God promiscuously and at random, use His Name with reverence when all the rest of their discourse is filled with froth and vanity? That Name is not to be sported with and tossed to and fro upon every light tongue. O my reader, form the habit of solemnly considering *whose* Name it is you are about to utter. It is the Name of Him who is present with you, who is hearing you pronounce it. He is jealous of His honor, and He will dreadfully avenge Himself upon those who have slighted Him.

God's Name is used in vain when it is employed *hypocritically*, when we profess to be His people and are not. Israel of old was guilty of this sin: "Hear ye this, O house of Jacob, which are called by the name of Israel, and are come forth out of the waters of Judah, which swear by the name of the Lord, and make mention of the God of Israel, *but not in truth,* nor in righteousness" (Isa. 48:1).

They used the Name of God, but did not obey the revelation contained therein, and so violated this Third Commandment (compare Matt. 7:22, 23). When using the Name of God, we must do so in a way which is true to its meaning and to its implications. Therefore He says to us, "Why call ye Me, Lord, Lord, *and do not* the things which I say?" (Luke 6:46). In like manner, we are guilty of this awful sin when we perform holy duties lightly and mechanically, our affections not being in them. Prayer without practice is blasphemy, and to speak to God with our lips while our hearts are far from Him is but a mocking of Him and an increasing of our condemnation.

God's Name is taken in vain when we swear lightly and irreverently, using the Name of God with as little respect as we would show to that of a man, or when we swear falsely and are guilty of perjury. When we are placed on oath and we attest that to be true which we do not know to be true, or which we know to be false, we are guilty of one of the gravest sins which man can possibly commit, for he has solemnly called upon the great God to witness that which the father of lies has prompted him to speak. "He that sweareth in the earth shall swear by *the God of Truth*" (Isa. 65:16), and therefore it behooves him to consider well whether what he testifies is true or not. Alas, oaths have become so excessively multiplied among us—being interwoven, as it were, into the body politic—and so generally disregarded, that the enormity of this offense is scarcely considered. "Let none of you imagine evil in your hearts against his neighbor; and love no *false oaths,* for all these are things that I *hate,* saith the Lord" (Zech. 8:17).

And what shall be said of that vast throng of profane swearers who pollute our language and wound our ears, by a vile mixture of execrations and blasphemies in their common conversation! "Their throat is an open sepulchre . . . the poison of asps is under their lips: whose mouth is full of cursing and bitterness" (Rom. 3:13, 14). Utterly vain is their thoughtless plea that they mean no harm, vain their excuse that all their companions do the same, vain their plea that it is merely to relieve their feelings! What a madness it is when men anger you, to strike against *God* and provoke Him far more than others can provoke you! But though their fellows do not censure, nor the police arrest, nor the magistrate punish them, yet *"The Lord* will not hold him guiltless that taketh his Name in vain." "As he loved cursing, so let it come unto him . . . as he clothed himself with cursing like as with his garment, so let it come into his bowels like water" (Psa. 109:17, 18). God is dreadfully incensed by this sin, and in the common commission of this Heaven-insulting crime our country has incurred terrible guilt.

It has become almost impossible to walk the streets or to enter mixed company without hearing the sacred Name of God treated with blasphemous contempt. The novels of the day, the stage, and even radio (and more lately television, the cinema, and the press) are terrible offenders, and without doubt this is one of the fearful sins against Himself for which God is now pouring out His judgments upon us. Of old He said unto Israel, *"Because of swearing* (cursing) *the land mourneth;* the pleasant places of the wilderness are dried up, and their course is evil" (Jer. 23:10). And He is still the same: "The Lord will not hold him guiltless that taketh His Name in vain." Sore punishment shall be his portion, if not in this life, then most assuredly so, eternally so, in the life to come.

THE FOURTH COMMANDMENT

"Remember the Sabbath day, to keep it holy. Six days shalt thou labour, and do all thy work; but the seventh day is the Sabbath of the Lord thy God; in it thou shalt not do any work" (Ex. 20:8-10). This commandment denotes that God is the sovereign Lord of *our time,* which is to be used and improved by us just as He has here specified. It is to be carefully noted that it consists of *two* parts, each of which bears directly upon the other. "Six days *shalt thou* (not "mayest thou") labour" is as Divinely binding upon us as "Remember the Sabbath day to keep it holy." It is a precept requiring us diligently to attend unto that vocation and state of life in which the Divine providence has placed us, to perform its offices with care and conscience. The revealed will of God is that man should work, not idle away his time; that he should work not five days a week (for which organized labor once agitated), but *six.*

He who never works is unfitted for worship. Work is to pave the way for worship, as worship is to fit us for work. The fact that any man can escape the observance of this first half of the Commandment is a sad reflection upon our modern social order, and shows how far we have departed from the Divine plan and ideal. The more diligent and faithful we are in performing the duties of the six days, the more shall we value the rest of the seventh. It will thus be seen that the appointing of the Sabbath was not any arbitrary restriction upon man's freedom, but a merciful provision for his good: that it is designed as a day of gladness and not of gloom. It is the Creator's gracious exempting us from our life of mundane toil one day in seven, granting us a foretaste of that future and better life for which the present is but a probation, when we may turn wholly from that which is material to that which is spiritual, and thereby be equipped for taking hold with new consecration and renewed energies upon the work of the coming days.

It should thus be quite evident that this law for the regulation of man's time was not a temporary one, designed for any particular dispensation, but is continuous and perpetual in the purpose of God: the Sabbath was "made for *man*" (Mark 2:27) and not simply for the Jew; it was made for man's good. What has been pointed out above upon the twofoldness of this Divine statute receives clear and irrefragable confirmation in the reason given for its enforcement: "for in six days the Lord made heaven and earth, the sea, and all that in them is, and rested the seventh day" (v. 11). Observe well the *twofoldedness* of this: the august Creator deigned to set an example before His creatures in each respect: HE worked for "six days," He "rested the seventh day!" It should also be pointed out that the appointing of work for man is not the consequence of sin: *before* the Fall, God put him "into the garden of Eden to *dress* and to *keep* it" (Gen. 2:15).

The lasting nature or perpetuity of this twofold Commandment is further evidenced by the fact that in the above reason given for its enforcement there was nothing which was peculiarly pertinent to the nation of Israel, but instead, that which speaks with clarion voice to the whole human race. Moreover, this statute was given a place not in the ceremonial law of Israel, which was to be done away when Christ fulfilled its types, but in the Moral Law, which was written by the finger of God Himself upon tables of stone, to signify to us its permanent nature. Finally, it should be pointed out that the very terms of this Commandment make it unmistakably plain that it was not designed only for the Jews, for it was equally binding upon any Gentiles who dwelt among them. Even though they were not in covenant with God, nor under the ceremonial law, yet they were required to keep the Sabbath holy—"thou shalt not do any work ... *nor thy stranger* that is within thy gates" (v. 10)!

"The seventh day is the Sabbath of the Lord thy God". Note well it is *not* said (here, or anywhere in Scripture) "the seventh day *of the week,*" but simply "the seventh day," that is, the day following the six of work. With the Jews it was the seventh day of the week, namely, Saturday, but for us it is—as the "another day" of Heb. 4:8 plainly intimates—the first day of the week, because the Sabbath not only commemorates the work of creation, but it now also celebrates the yet greater work of redemption. Thus, the Lord so worded the fourth Commandment as to suit *both* the Jewish and the Christian dispensations, and thereby intimated its perpetuity. The Christian Sabbath is from midnight Saturday to midnight Sunday: it is clear from John 20:1 that it began *before* sunrise, and therefore we may conclude it starts at Saturday midnight; while from John 20:19 we learn (from the fact it is not there called "the evening of the second day") that it continues throughout the evening, and that our worship is also to continue therein.

But though the Christian Sabbath does not commence till midnight on Saturday, yet our *preparation for it* must begin sooner, or how else can we obey its express requirement, "in it thou shalt not do any work"? On the Sabbath there is to be a complete resting the whole day, not only from natural recreations and doing our own pleasure (Isa. 58:13), but from all worldly employment. The wife needs a day of rest just as much as her husband, yea, being the "weaker vessel," more so. Such things as porridge and soup can be prepared on the Saturday and heated on the Sabbath, so that we may be entirely free to delight ourselves in the Lord and give ourselves completely to His worship and service. Let us also see to it that we do not work or sit up so late on the Saturday night that we encroach on the Lord's day by staying late in bed or making ourselves drowsy for its holy duties.

This Commandment makes it clear that God is to be worshipped *in the home*, which, of course, inculcates the practice of family worship. It is addressed more specifically than any of the other nine Commandments to heads of households and to employers, because God requires them to see to it that all under their charge shall observe the Sabbath. To them, more immediately, God says, "Remember the Sabbath day to keep it holy." It is to be strictly set apart to the honor of the thrice holy God, spent in the exercises of holy contemplation, meditation, and adoration. Because it is the day which He has made (Psa. 118:24), we must do nothing to unmake it. This Commandment forbids the omission of any duties required, a careless performing of the same, or a weariness in them. The more faithfully we keep *this* Commandment, the better prepared shall we be to obey the other nine.

Three classes of works, and three only, may be engaged in on the "Holy Sabbath." Works of *necessity*, which are those that could not be done on the preceding day and that cannot be deferred till the next—such as tending to cattle. Works of *mercy*, which are those that compassion requires us to perform toward other creatures—such as ministering to the sick. Works of *piety*, which are the worship of God in public and in private, using with thankfulness and delight all the means of grace which He has provided. We need to watch and strive against the very first suggestions of Satan to corrupt our hearts, divert our minds, or disturb us in holy duties, praying earnestly for help to meditate upon God's Word and to retain what He gives us. The Lord makes the sacred observance of His Day of special blessing; and contrariwise, He visits the profanation of the Sabbath with special cursing (see Neh. 13:17, 18), as our guilty land is now proving to its bitter cost.

> "A Sabbath well spent, brings a week of content
> And strength for the toils of the morrow;
> But a Sabbath profaned, whate'er may be gained
> Is a certain forerunner of sorrow."

THE FIFTH COMMANDMENT

This commandment to honor parents is much broader in its scope than appears at first glance. It is not to be restricted to our literal *father* and *mother,* but is to be applied to all our superiors. "The end of the Precept is, that since the Lord God desires the preservation of the order He has appointed, the degrees of preeminence fixed by Him ought to be inviolably preserved. The sum of it therefore will be that we should reverence them whom God has exalted to any authority over us, and should render them honor, obedience, and gratitude. . . . But as this precept is exceedingly repugnant to the depravity of human nature, whose ardent desire of exaltation will scarcely admit of subjection, it has therefore proposed as an example that kind of superiority which is naturally most amiable and least invidious, because that might the more easily mollify and incline our minds to a habit of submission" (Calvin).

Lest any of our readers—in this socialistic and communistic age, when insubordination and lawlessness is the evil spirit of our day—object to this wider interpretation of the commandment, let us ponder the following considerations. First, "honor" belongs primarily and principally to God. Secondarily, and by derivation, it pertains also to those whom He has dignified and made nobles in His kingdom, by raising them above others and bestowing titles and dominion upon them. We ought to revere these just as surely as we do our fathers and mothers. In Scrip-

ture the word "honor" has an extensive application, as
may be seen from I Tim. 5:17; I Pet. 2:17, etc. Secondly,
observe that the title "father" is given to kings (I Sam.
24:11; Isa. 49:23), masters (II Kings 5:13), and ministers
of the Gospel (II Kings 2:12; Gal. 4:19).

"Wherefore it ought not be doubted that God here lays
down a universal rule for our conduct, namely, that to every one whom we know to be placed in authority over us
by His appointment, we should render reverence, obedience, gratitude, and all the other services in our power.
Nor does it make any difference whether they are worthy
of this honor or not. For whatever be their characters, yet
it is not without the appointment of the Divine providence
that they have attained that station on account of which
the supreme Legislator has commanded them to be honored. He has particularly enjoined reverence to our parents, who have brought us into this life" (Calvin). It
scarcely needs to be said that the duty enforced here is of a
reciprocal nature, those of *inferiors* implying a corresponding obligation on *superiors;* but limited space obliges us to
consider here only the duties resting on subjects to their
rulers.

First let us consider the duties of *children to their
parents.* They are to love and reverence them, being fearful of offending due to the respect they bear them. A gen-
uine filial veneration is to actuate children, so that they
abstain from whatever would grieve or offend their
parents. They are to be subject unto them: mark the
blessed example which Christ has left (Luke 2:51). "Children obey your parents in all things, for this is well pleasing unto the Lord" (Col. 3:20). After David was anointed
for the throne, he fulfilled his father's appointment by
tending his sheep (I Sam. 16:19). They are to hearken to
their instructions and imitate their godly practices (Prov.
6:20). Their language must ever be respectful and their
gestures betoken submission. Though Joseph was so

highly exalted in Egypt, he "bowed himself with his face to the ground" before his father (Gen. 48:12). And note how king Solomon honored his mother (I Kings 2:19). As far as they are able and their parents have need, they are to provide for them in old age (I Tim. 5:16).

Secondly, let us observe *our duties to rulers and magistrates* whom God has set over us. These are God's deputies and vicegerents, being invested with authority from Him: "by Me kings reign" (Prov. 8:15). God has ordained civil authority for the general good of mankind, for were it not for this men would be savage beasts preying upon one another. Did not the fear of magistrates restrain those who have cast off the fear of God, were they not afraid of temporal punishments, we should be as safe among lions and tigers as among men. Rulers are to be honored in our thoughts, regarding them as the official representatives of God upon earth (Eccl. 10:20; Rom. 13:1ff; Acts 23:5). They are to be revered in our speeches, supporting their office and authority, for of the wicked it is written, "they are not afraid to speak evil of dignities" (II Pet. 2:20). We are to obey them. "Submit yourselves to every ordinance of man for the Lord's sake: whether it be to the king, as supreme; or unto governors, as unto them that are sent by him for the punishment of evildoers, and for the praise of them that do well" (I Pet. 2:13, 14). We are to render "tribute to whom tribute is due, custom to whom custom, fear to whom fear; honour to whom honour" (Rom. 13:7). We are to pray for them (I Tim. 2:1, 2).

Thirdly, let us consider the duties of *servants unto their masters*. They are to obey them. "Servants obey in all things your masters according to the flesh: not with eyeservice as menpleasers, but in singleness of heart fearing God" (Col. 3:22). They are to be diligent in duty, seeking to promote their master's interests, "showing all good fidelity" (Titus 2:10; and see Eph. 6:5-7). They are to patiently suffer their rebukes and corrections, "not answering again" (Titus 2:9). So strictly has God enjoined them to a quiet submission to their masters that, even when a servant has given no just cause for rebuke, yet he is to silently suffer the groundless anger of his master. "Servants be subject to your masters with all fear: not only to the good and gentle, but also to the froward. For this is thankworthy, if a man for conscience toward God endure grief, suffering wrongfully" (I Pet. 2:18-20). O how far have we wandered from the Divine standard!

Finally, we should mention *pastors and their flocks,* ministers and their people, for between them also is such a relation of superiors and inferiors as brings them under the direction of this fifth commandment. "Obey them that have the rule over you, and submit yourselves: for they watch for your souls, as they that must give account, that they may do it with joy, and not with grief: for that is unprofitable for you" (Heb. 13:17). Christ has so vested his servants with authority that He declares, "He that heareth you heareth Me; and he that despiseth you despiseth Me" (Luke 10:16). So again, "Let the elders that rule well be counted worthy of double honour, especially they who labour in the Word and doctrine" (I Tim. 5:17). This "double honour" is that of reverence and maintenance. "Let him that is taught in the Word communicate unto him that teacheth in all good things" (Gal. 6:6 and cf. I Cor. 9:11). How solemn is this warning: "But they mocked the messengers of God and despised His words and misused His prophets, until the wrath of the Lord arose against His people, till there was no remedy" (II Chron. 36 :16).

To this precept is added this promise as a motive and encouragement to obedience: "That thy days may be long upon the land which the Lord thy God giveth thee." First, as an Old Testament promise this is to be regarded typically of the Eternal Life promised by the Gospel, since Canaan was a figure of Heaven. Secondly, it is repeated in the New Testament (Eph. 6:2, 3 and I Pet. 3:10), since it is often God's way to lengthen out an obedient and holy life. Thirdly, all promises of earthly blessing, however, must necessarily imply this condition: they shall be literally fulfilled to us if this would promote our eternal happiness—otherwise they would be threatenings and not promises. In His mercy God often abridges this promise and takes His beloved home to Himself.

THE SIXTH COMMANDMENT

"Thou shalt not kill" (Ex. 20:13). In the first five Commandments we have seen how God safeguarded His own glory; in the second five we are to behold how He provides for the security and well-being of men: (1) for the protection of man's person; (2) for the sanctity and good of his family ("thou shalt not commit adultery"); (3) for the safety of his estate and substance ("thou shalt not steal"); (4) for his reputation or good name ("thou shalt not bear false witness against thy neighbour"). Finally, as a strong fence encircling the whole Law, God not only prohibits outward crimes, but inward motions of evil in our thoughts and affections ("thou shalt not covet"). It is the first of these regulations which specially relates to our neighbor that we shall now consider: "thou shalt not kill."

This sixth Commandment prohibits that barbarous and inhuman sin of murder, which is the firstborn of the Devil, who was "a murderer from the beginning" (John 8:44). It is the first crime we read of after the fall of Adam and Eve, wherein the corruption transmitted to their descendants was fearfully displayed by Cain. His rancor and enmity goaded him to slay Abel, because his brother's "works were righteous and his own evil" (I John 3:12). But this commandment is not restricted to forbidding the actual crime of murder. It also prohibits all the degrees and causes of murder, such as rash anger and hatred, slanders and revenge, and whatever else may prejudice the safety of our neighbor or tempt us to see him perish when it is in our power to relieve and rescue him.

Let us begin by pointing out that every killing of a man is not murder. It is not so in the execution of justice, when the magistrate sentences a slayer, for he is vested with lawful authority to put capital offenders to death, and if he fails to do so, then God will charge it upon him as sin. "Whoso sheddeth man's blood, by man shall his blood be shed" (Gen. 9:6). These words state the general and unchanging principle. "Thine eye shall not pity, but life shall go for life" (Deut. 19:21). This is God's order to the magistrate. Nor is the shedding of blood in a righteous war chargeable with murder. It is lawful to take up arms against an invader and to recover what has been unjustly taken away. Thus David pursued the Amalekites who had carried away his wives captive. It is also lawful in order to punish some great injury or wrong. David made war upon the Ammonites for their outraging of his ambassadors (II Sam. 10).

As there are some who decry this assertion and denounce all war as unlawful in this Christian dispensation, let us point out that when soldiers came to Christ's forerunner for instruction saying, "What shall we do?" (Luke 3:14), he did not say, Fight no more, abandon your calling, but gave them directions how they should conduct themselves. When the centurion came to the Savior and drew arguments from his military calling, our Lord did not condemn his profession or rebuke him for holding such an office. Instead, He highly commended his faith (Luke 7:8, 9). When examined by Pilate Christ declared, "My kingdom is not of this world: if My kingdom were of this world, then would My servants fight, that I should not be delivered to the Jews: but now is My kingdom not from hence" (John 18:36). Those words clearly imply that though carnal means were improper for advancing Christ's spiritual kingdom, yet had not His state of humiliation prevented His assuming the royal scepter, His followers might lawfully have fought to defend His title.

There is one other exception, namely, accidental slaying, which is not chargeable with murder, that is, when life is taken without any intention of so doing. Such a case we find mentioned in Scripture, as when hewing wood the axe should slip and undesignedly kill a neighbor (Deut. 19:5). For such innocent slayers the Lord appointed cities of refuge, whither they could find safe asylum from the avenger of blood. But let it be pointed out that we must be employed about *lawful* things. Otherwise, if we are engaged in what is unjustified and it leads to the death of another, this cannot be excused from murder (see Ex. 21:22-24).

Next let us consider cases of murder. Suicide is *self-murder*, and is one of the most desperate crimes which can be committed. Inasmuch as this sin precludes repentance on the part of its perpetrator, it is beyond forgiveness. Such creatures are so abandoned by God as to have no concern for their eternal salvation, seeing they pass into the immediate presence of their Judge with their hands imbrued in their own blood. Such are self-murderers, for they destroy not only their bodies but their souls, too. The murdering *of another* is a most heinous crime. It torments the conscience of its perpetrator with fearful affrights, so that often he gives himself up to justice. Those who are *accessories* are also guilty of murder, such as those who commission it to be done (II Sam. 11:15; 12:9), or consent thereto (as Pilate), or conceal it (as in Deut. 21:6, 7, by clear implication).

This Commandment not only forbids the perpetration of murder, but likewise all causes and occasions leading to it. The principal of these are envy and anger. Envy has been well described as "the rust of a cankered soul, a foul vice which turns the happiness of others into our own misery." Cain first enviously repined at the success of his brother's sacrifice, and this quickly prompted him to murder. So too unjust and inordinate anger, if it be allowed to lie festering in the heart, will turn into the venom of an implacable hatred. Such anger is not only a cause, but it is actually a degree of murder, as is clear from the teaching of Christ in Matt. 5:21, 22.

It should be pointed out that anger is not, as envy, simply, and in itself, unlawful. There is a virtuous anger, which (so far from being sin, is a noble and praiseworthy grace, see Mark 3:5). To be moved with indignation for the cause of God when his glory is degraded, His name dishonored, His sanctuary polluted, and His people vilified is a holy anger. So there is an innocent and allowable anger when we are unjustly provoked by offenses against ourselves, but here we need to be much on our guard that we "sin not" (Eph. 4:26). A vicious and sinful anger, which darkens the understanding and makes one act as in a frenzy, is one which is without cause and without bounds. Jonah 4:1 gives an illustration of a groundless anger. Anger is *immoderate* when it is violent and excessive, or when it continues to boil. "Let not the sun go down on your wrath" (Eph. 4:26); if it does, the scum of malice will be on your heart next morning!

In closing, let us give some rules for restraining and repressing anger. (1) Labor and pray for a meek and humble spirit. Think lowly of yourself and you will not be angered if others slight you. All contention proceeds from pride (Prov. 13:10). The more you despise yourself the easier it will be to bear the contempt of your fellows. (2) Think often of the infinite patience and forbearance of God. How many affronts does He bear with from us. How often we give Him occasion to be angry with us, yet "He hath not dealt with us after our sins." Let this great example be ours. (3) Beware of prejudice against any, for it is sure to misinterpret their actions. Fight against the first risings of envy and anger; when injured put it down to ignorance or unintention. (4) Shun angry persons (Prov. 22:24, 25) ; fire quickly spreads.

THE SEVENTH COMMANDMENT

"Thou shalt not commit adultery" (Ex. 20:14). The virtues of purity are the basis of the domestic relations, and as the family is the foundation of human society, the class of duties here involved is second only to those which preserve man's existence. Hence it is that, immediately following the commandment which declares the sacredness of human life, there is that precept that is a hedge about the highest relationship of creaturehood, thus safeguarding the holy function of the procreation of life. Nothing is more essential for the social order than that the relationship upon which all others are subsequently based should be jealously protected against every form of attack. The commandment is a simple, unqualified, irrevocable negative: "thou shalt not." No argument is used, no reason is given, because none is required. This sin is so destructive and damning that the mere mention of its name is, in itself, sufficient cause for this stern forbidding.

This commandment plainly intimates that God claims *the body* as well as the soul for His service. "I beseech you therefore, brethren, by the mercies of God, that ye present your bodies a living sacrifice, holy, acceptable unto God, which is your reasonable service" (Rom. 12:1). "Let not sin therefore reign in your mortal body, that ye should obey it in the lusts thereof. . . . if ye through the Spirit do mortify the deeds of the body, ye shall live" (Rom. 6:12; 8:13). "The body is not for fornication, but for the Lord; and the Lord for the body. . . . Know ye not that your bodies are the members of Christ? shall I then take the members of Christ, and make them the members of a harlot? God forbid. . . . glorify God in your body, and in your spirit" (I Cor. 6:13, 15, 20). For a Christian, this foul sin is sacrilege. "Know ye not that your body is the temple of the holy Spirit which is in you. . .?" (I Cor. 6:19). If Christ was indignant when He saw the house of God turned into a den of thieves, how much more heinous in His sight must be that wickedness which debases the temple of the Holy Spirit into a filthy sty!

"Thou shalt not commit adultery." This prohibition is designed to guard the sanctity of the home, for strictly speaking "adultery" is a crime which none but a *married* person can commit—"fornication" being the name of it when done by one who is single. As the One with whom we have to do is ineffably pure and holy, therefore does He require us to depart from all uncleanness. This commandment respects more especially the government of the affections and passions, the keeping of our minds and bodies in such a chaste frame that nothing impure or immodest may defile us. It requires the proper discipline of those inclinations which God has implanted for the increase of the human species. Therefore we are to avoid everything that may be an occasion of this sin, using all proper means and methods to prevent all temptations thereto.

How *God* regards sins of uncleanness has been made clear by many passages in His Word. This sin, even on the part of an unmarried man, is called "great wickedness against God" (Gen. 39:9). Then how much more inexcusable and intolerable is it on the part of a married person! The temporal punishment meted out to it under the civil law of Israel was no less than death, the same that was meted out to murder. Job calls it "a heinous crime, a fire that consumeth to destruction" (31:11, 12). Much of this wickedness is practiced in secret, but though its perpetrators may escape the judgment of man, they shall not escape the judgment of Heaven, for it is written, "whoremongers and adulterers *God* shall judge" (Heb. 13:4). "Be not deceived: neither fornicators, nor idolators, nor adulterers . . . shall inherit the kingdom of God" (I Cor. 6:9, 10).

"The sin of adultery is scarcely less enormous than that of murder. The latter destroys man's temporal existence, the former destroys all that makes existence a boon. Were all to take the licence of the adulterer men would in due time be reduced to the degradation of wild beasts" (R. L. Dabney). To prevent this sin, God has instituted the ordinance of marriage. "To avoid fornication, let every man have his own wife, and let every woman have her own husband" (I Cor. 7:2). The sin of adultery is therefore the violation of the marriage covenant and vow, and so adds perjury to infidelity. Immorality is a sin against the body (I Cor. 6:18). God's displeasure against this sin is seen in the fact that He has so ordered things that nature itself visits the same with heavy penalties in every part of man's complex being. "Be not deceived: God is not mocked: for whatsoever a man soweth, that shall he also reap. For he that soweth to his flesh shall of the flesh reap corruption" (Gal. 6:7, 8).

Though marriage is the Divinely appointed remedy for the sin of sexual uncleanness, that does not grant man the license to make a beast of himself. "Let it not be supposed by married persons that all things are lawful to them. Every man should observe sobriety towards his wife, and every wife, reciprocally, towards her husband; conducting themselves in such a manner as to do nothing unbecoming the decorum and temperance of marriage. For thus ought marriage contracted in the Lord to be regulated by moderation and modesty, and not to break out into the vilest lasciviousness. Such sensuality has been stigmatized by Ambrose with a severe but not unmerited

censure, when he calls those who in their conjugal inter-
course have no regard to modesty, the adulterers of their
own wives" (Calvin).

Let no man flatter himself with the idea that he cannot
be charged with unchastity because he has abstained from
the actual deed while his heart is a cesspool of defiling
imaginations and desires. Because God's Law is "spiritual" (Rom. 7:14), it not only forbids the gross outward
acts of filthiness, but it prohibits and condemns unchastity
of heart as well—all unlawful imaginations and contem-
plations. As there is such a thing as *heart murder,* so
there is *heart adultery,* and he who commits speculative
uncleanness and prostitutes his thoughts and imaginations
to the impure embraces of lust is guilty of transgressing
this commandment. "Whosoever looketh on a woman to
lust after her hath committed adultery with her already
in his heart" (Matt. 5:28). Therefore we find the Apostle
did not content himself with saying that it is better for a
man to marry than to pollute himself with a harlot, but
"it is better to marry than to *burn*" (I Cor. 7:9) —harbor
consuming passion.

Although the sin of "adultery" is alone specifically
mentioned in this precept, the rules by which these Commandments are to be interpreted (see earlier chapters)
oblige us to understand that all other kinds of uncleanness are prohibited under that of this one gross sin. Everything that defiles the body is here forbidden; adultery is
expressly mentioned because all other moral pollutions
tend thereto. By the wickedness of that which all men
know to be wrong, we are exhorted to abominate *every*
unlawful passion. As all manner of chastity in our
thoughts, speeches, and actions is enjoined by the perfect
rule of God, so whatever is in the least contrary and prej-
udicial to spotless chastity and modesty is here prohibited.
Every other sexual union save that of marriage is ac-
cursed in God's sight.

This commandment forbids all degrees or approaches to the sin prohibited, as looking in order to lust. Its force is, Thou shalt in no way injure thy neighbor's chastity or tempt to uncleanness. It requires that we abstain from immodest apparel, indelicate speech, intemperance in food and drink which excites the passions, and everything that has any tendency to induce unchastity in ourselves or others. Let young people especially fix it in mind that all unclean conduct *before* marriage on the part of man or woman is a wrong done *against* the marriage to be. Though this commandment is expressed in the form of a negative prohibition, yet positively it enjoins all the opposite duties, such as cleanliness of the body, filling the mind with holy objects, setting our affection on things above, and spending our time in profitable occupations.

Rules and Helps for Avoiding Such Sins

(1) Cultivate a habitual sense of the Divine presence, realizing that "The eyes of the Lord are in *every* place, beholding the evil and the good" (Prov. 15:3). (2) Keep a strict watch over the senses, for these are the avenues which instead of letting in pleasant streams to refresh, only too often let in mud and mire to pollute the soul. Make a covenant with your eyes (Job 31:1). Stop your ears against all filthy conversation. Read nothing which defiles. Watch your thoughts, and labor promptly to expel evil ones. (3) Practice sobriety and temperance (I Cor. 9:27). Those who indulge in gluttony and drunkenness generally find that their excesses froth and foam into lust. (4) Exercise yourself in honest and lawful employment; idleness proves as fatal to many as intemperance to others. Avoid the company of the wicked. (5) Be much in earnest prayer, begging God to cleanse your heart (Psa. 119:37).

"Ye adulterers and adulteresses, know ye not that the friendship of the world is enmity with God?" (James 4:4).

This refers to the sin of *spiritual adultery*: it is love of the world estranging the heart from God, carnal lusts enticing the soul and drawing it away from Him. There is more than enough in God Himself to satisfy, but there is still that in the believer which desires to find his happiness in the creature. There are *degrees* of this sin, as of the natural. As there may be physical adultery in thought and longing that terminates not in the overt act, so the Christian may secretly hanker after the world though he become not an utter worldling. We must check such inclinations when our hearts are unduly drawn forth to material comforts and contentments. God is a jealous God, and nothing provokes Him more than that we should prefer base things before Himself, or give to others that affection or esteem which belongs alone to Him. Leave not your "first love" (Rev. 2:4), nor forsake Him to whom you are "espoused" (II Cor. 11:2).

THE EIGHTH COMMANDMENT

"Thou shalt not steal" (Ex. 20:15). The root from which theft proceeds is *discontent* with the portion God has allotted, and therefrom a coveting of what He has withheld from us and bestowed upon others. With his usual accuracy Calvin hit the nail on the head when he wrote, "This law is ordained for our hearts as much as for our hands, in order that men may study both to protect the property and to promote the interests of others." Like the preceding one, this precept also respects the government of our affections, by the setting of due bounds to our desires after worldly things, that they may not exceed what the good providence of God has appointed us. Hence the suitability of that prayer, "Remove far from me vanity and lies: give me neither poverty nor riches, feed me with food convenient for me; lest I be full and deny Thee, and say, Who is the Lord? or lest I be poor, and steal, and take the name of my God in vain" (Prov. 30:8, 9).

"Thou shalt not steal." The positive duty here enjoined is this: thou shalt by all proper means preserve and further both thine own and thy neighbor's estate. This commandment requires proper diligence and industry so as to secure a competency for ourselves and families, that we may not through our own default expose ourselves and them to those straits which are the consequence of sloth and neglect. Thus we are to "provide things honest in the sight of all men" (Rom. 12:17). But even more, this commandment is the law of love with respect to our neighbor's estate. It requires honesty and uprightness in our dealings one with another, being founded upon that first practical principle of all human conduct: "Whatsoever ye would that men should do to you, do ye even so to them" (Matt. 7:12). Thus this commandment places a sacred enclosure around property which none can lawfully enter without the proprietor's consent.

The solemn and striking fact deserves pointing out that the first sin committed by the human species entailed *theft*: Eve took of (stole) the forbidden fruit. So, too, the first recorded sin against Israel after they entered the land of Canaan was that of theft: Achan stole from among the spoils (Josh. 7:21). In like manner the first sin which defiled the primitive Christian church was theft: Ananias and Sapphira "kept back part of the price" (Acts 5:2). How often this is the first sin committed outwardly by children! And therefore this Divine precept should be taught to them from earliest infancy. Years ago we visited a home, and our hostess related how she had that day secretly observed her daughter (about four years old) enter a room in which was a large bunch of grapes. The little tot eyed them longingly, went up to the table and then said, "Get thee hence, Satan. It is written, 'Thou shalt not steal,' " and rushed out of the room.

"Thou shalt not steal." The highest form of this sin is where it is committed against *God,* which is sacrilege. Of old He charged Israel with this crime: "Will a man rob God? yet ye have robbed Me. But ye say, Wherein have we robbed Thee? In tithes and offerings. Ye are cursed with a curse: for ye have robbed Me, even this whole nation" (Mal. 3:8,9). But there are other ways in which this wickedness may be committed besides that of refusing to financially support the maintenance of God's cause on earth. God is robbed when we withhold from Him the glory which is His due, and we are spiritual thieves when we arrogate to ourselves the honor and praise which belong to Him alone. Arminians are great offenders here, by ascribing to free will what is produced by free grace. "Ye have not chosen Me," said Christ, "but I have chosen you" (John 15:16). "Herein is love, not that we loved God, but that He loved us" (I John 4:10).

Another way in which we rob God is by an unfaithful discharge of our stewardship. That which God has entrusted to us may be just as really outraged by our mismanagement as if we interfered with another's trust or plundered our neighbor's goods. This commandment then requires from us that we administer our worldly estate, be it large or small, with such industry as to provide for ourselves and those dependent upon us. Idleness is a species of theft. It is playing the part of the drone and compelling the rest of the hive to support us. So prodigality is also a form of theft, since extravagance and wastefulness are a spending of that substance which God has divided to us in "riotous living." He who remains in secular employment that requires him to work on the Lord's Day is robbing God of the time which ought to be devoted to His worship. Before passing on it should be pointed out that one who obtrudes himself into the Gospel ministry without being called of God in order to obtain an easy and comfortable living is "a thief and a robber" (John 10:1).

God has ordained that men should earn their bread by the sweat of their brow, and with that portion which we thus honestly obtain, we must be satisfied. But some are slothful and refuse to labor, while others are covetous and crave a larger portion. Hence many are led to resort to the use of force or fraud in order to gain possession of that to which they have no right. Theft, in general, is an unjust taking or keeping to ourselves what is lawfully another's. He is a thief who withholds what ought to be in his neighbor's possession just as much as one who takes his neighbor's property from him. Hence this commandment is grossly violated both by management and labor. If in the past the poor have been wronged by inadequate wages, the scales have now turned in the opposite direction, when employees often demand a wage that industry cannot afford to pay them. If on the one hand it is right that a fair day's work should receive a fair day's pay, it holds equally true that a fair day's pay is entitled to a fair day's work. But where loafing obtains it does not receive it.

"Thou shalt not steal." Lying advertisements are a breach of this commandment. Tradesmen are guilty when they adulterate or misrepresent their goods, and also when they deliberately give short weight or short change to their customers. Profiteering is another form of theft. The Apostle Paul admonishes "that no man *go beyond* and defraud his brother in any matter" (I Thess. 4:6). The contracting of debts to support luxury and vanity is theft, as also is the failure to pay debts incurred in procuring necessities. A man is a thief in the sight of God who transfers property to his wife just before he becomes bankrupt, and so also is any bankrupt who later on prospers financially and then fails to pay his creditors to the full. That man or woman is a thief who borrows and returns not. This commandment is broken by tenants who heedlessly damage the property and furniture of the owner. Evasion in paying taxes is another form of theft; Christ has set us a better example (Matt. 17:24). Gambling is still another form of theft, for by it men obtain money for which they have done no honest work.

This old saying is true. "Whatever is gotten over the Devil's back goes under the Devil's belly." Certain it is that God sends a curse upon what is obtained by force or fraud: it is put into a bag with holes and under Providence soon wastes away. God, by His righteous judgment, often makes one sin the punisher of another and what is gained by theft is lost by intemperance and a short-ened life. Therefore it is written, "The robbery of the wicked shall destroy them" (Prov. 21:7); and again, "As the partridge sitteth on eggs and hatcheth them not; so he that getteth riches, and not by right, shall leave them in the midst of his days, and at his end shall be a fool" (Jer. 17:11). Many times God raises up those who deal with them as they have dealt with others. The fearful increase of this crime in modern society is due to failure to impose adequate punishment. If the reader is conscious of having wronged others in the past, it is not sufficient to confess this sin to God. At least a twofold *restitution* must be made (Luke 19:8 and II Sam. 12:6) —if the owner is dead, then to his descendants; if he has none, then to some public charity.

Here are a few suggested helps and aids to the avoidance of the sins prohibited and to the performance of those duties inculcated by this eighth commandment. (1) Engage in honest labor, or if a person of means, in some honorable calling, seeking to promote the public good. It is idle people who are most tempted to mischief. (2) Strive against the spirit of selfishness by seeking the welfare of others. (3) Counter the lust of covetousness by giving liberally to those in need. (4) If your Savior was crucified between two thieves that the gift of salvation might be yours, bring no reproach upon His name by any act of dishonesty. (5) Cultivate the grace of contentment. In order thereto, consider frequently the vanity of all things temporal, practice submission to Divine prov-idence, meditate much on the Divine promises (such as Heb. 13:5, 6), be temperate in all things, set your affec-tions on things above, and remind yourself daily of the earthly lot of Christ.

THE NINTH COMMANDMENT

"Thou shalt not bear false witness against thy neighbour" (Ex. 20:16). Take these words simply at their face value and they prohibit only the horrible crime of perjury or the giving of false testimony in a court of law. But as with the previous Commandments, so it is here: much more is implied and inculcated than is specifically stated. As we have so often pointed out, each of the Ten Commandments enunciates a general principle, and not only are all other sins forbidden which be allied to the one named and prohibited, together with all causes and tendencies thereto, but the opposite virtue is definitely required, with all that fosters and promotes it. Thus, in its wider meaning, this ninth commandment reprehends any word of ours which would injure the reputation of our neighbor, be it uttered in public or in private. This should scarcely need any arguing, for if we restrict this commandment to its literal terms it would have no bearing on any save that small minority who are called upon to bear witness in a court of justice.

In its widest application this commandment has to do with the regulation of our *speech,* which is one of the distinguishing and ennobling faculties that God has bestowed upon man. Scripture tells us that "death and life are in the power of the tongue" (Prov. 18:21), that "a wholesome tongue is a tree of life" (Prov. 15:4), and that an unbridled one is "an unruly evil, full of deadly poison" (James 3:8). That our words are not to be uttered lightly or thoughtlessly is made clear by that unspeakably solemn utterance of our Lord's: "But I say unto you, That every idle word that men shall speak, they shall give account thereof in the day of judgment. For by thy words thou shalt be justified, and by thy words thou shalt be condemned" (Matt. 12: 36, 37). O how we need to pray, "Set a watch, O Lord, before my mouth; keep the door of my lips" (Psa. 141:3). The duties concerning our tongues may be summed up in two words: our speech must always be *true* and spoken *in love* (Eph. 4:15). Thus, as the eighth commandment provides for the security of our neighbor's property, so this one is designed to preserve his good name by our speaking the truth about him in love.

Negatively, this ninth commandment forbids all false and injurious speeches respecting our neighbor; positively, it inculcates the conservation of *truth*. "The end of this Precept is that because God, who is Truth itself, execrates a lie, we ought to preserve the truth without the least disguise" (Calvin). Veracity is the strict observance of truth in all our communications. The importance and necessity of this appears from the fact that almost all that mankind knows is derived from communications. The value of those statements which we accept from others depends entirely on their verity and accuracy. If they are false, they are worthless, misleading, and evil. Veracity is not only a virtue, but it is also the root of all other virtues and the foundation of all right character. In Scripture, therefore, "truth" is often synonymous with "righteousness." The godly man is "he that speaketh truth in his heart" (Psa. 15:2). The man that "doeth truth" (John 3:21) has discharged his duty. It is by the *truth* that the Holy Spirit sanctifies the soul (John 17:17).

The positive form of this ninth commandment is found in these words: "Speak ye every man the truth to his neighbour" (Zech. 8:16). Thus the first sin prohibited therein is that of *lying*. Now a lie, properly speaking, consists of three elements or ingredients: speaking what is not true; deliberately doing so; and doing so with an intent to deceive. Every falsehood is not a lie; we may be misinformed or deceived and sincerely think we are stating facts, and consequently have no design of misleading others. On the other hand, we may speak that which is true and yet lie in so doing, as in the following examples: we might report what is true, yet believe it to be false and utter it with an intention to deceive; or we might report the figurative words of another and pretend he meant them literally, as was the case with those who bore false witness against Christ (Matt. 26:60). The worst form of lying (between men) is when we maliciously invent a falsehood for the purpose of damaging the reputation of our neighbor, which is what is more especially in view in the terms of the ninth commandment.

How vile and abominable this sin is appears from the following considerations. It is a sin which makes a person most like the Devil. The Devil is a spirit, and therefore gross carnal sins do not correspond to his nature. His sins are more refined and intellectual, such as pride and malice, deception and falsehood. "He is a liar and the father of it" (John 8:44), and the more malice enters into one composition of any lie, the more nearly one resembles him. It is therefore a sin most contrary to the nature and character of God, for He is "the Lord God of truth" (Psa. 31:5), and therefore we are told that "lying lips are an abomination unto the Lord" (Prov. 12:22). As Satan is a liar and the father of lies, and as God is the Lord God of Truth, so His children resemble Him therein, "seeing they are My people, children that will not lie" (Isa. 63:8). God has threatened a most fearful punishment upon them; "all liars shall have their part in the lake which burneth with fire and brimstone" (Rev. 21:8).

Alas, to what fearful heights has this sin risen. It has become so common that few indeed have any conscience thereon, until we have to lament that "truth is fallen in the street" (Isa. 59:14). First, truth has departed from the pulpits. A whole century has passed since the lie of evolution captivated the scientific world and then was taken up by thousands of unregenerate preachers—a lie which strikes at the very foundations of Truth, for it repudiates man's fall, and sets aside his need both of redemption and regeneration. For the same length of time the so-called "higher criticism" of German neologians has been peddled throughout the English-speaking world by thousands of godless ministers, who wish to be looked up to as men of superior intellectuality. Once Truth departed from the pulpits it was not long before it departed from the halls of legislation and the marts of commerce, until we now live in a world where confidence between nations is non-existent, and where the word of our fellows is no longer to be relied upon.

How deeply important it is, then, that a sacred regard for the truth should be constantly pressed upon the young and that they should be taught that lying is the inlet of all vice and corruption. Equally important is it that those who have charge of the young, particularly their parents, should set before the little ones a personal example of what they teach, and not neutralize the same by making promises to them that they fail to fulfill or by uttering threats that they never carry out. It is the part of wisdom and prudence that each of us should be very slow in making an unconditional promise; but once it is made it must be kept at all costs, unless the keeping of it compels us to sin against God. The prohibition of bearing false witness against my neighbor equally forbids me to bear false witness about myself, which is done when I pose as being holier than I am or when I pretend to be more humble or more anything else than is actually the case.

It remains for us to point out that we may violate this ninth commandment even when we speak the truth, if we speak it unnecessarily and from improper motives. "We injure the character of our neighbor when we retail his real faults without any call to divulge them, when we relate them to those who have no right to know them, and when we tell them not to promote any good end but to make him lose his estimation in society.... Nay, we transgress this precept when we do not speak at all, for by holding our peace when something injurious is said of another we tacitly give our assent, and by concealing what we know to the contrary" (John Dick). Flattering a person is another form of violating this precept. To compliment another merely for the sake of pleasing him or gratifying his vanity is to perjure your soul and imperil his safety. So also to give a false testimony of character or to recommend a friend to another when we know him to be unworthy of the testimonial is to bear "false witness."

The following directions, through the grace of God, may be helpful in preserving one from these common sins. (1) Be not swayed by party spirit if you would be kept from slandering others. The spirit of sectarianism begets prejudice, and prejudice makes us unwilling to receive and to acknowledge good in those who walk not with us, and ready to believe the worst of them. How often writers are guilty here. Denominational bigotry has caused many a man to misinterpret one who differs with him and to impute to him errors which he does not hold. (2) Be not busy in other men's affairs; attend to your own business and leave others for God to attend to. (3) Reflect much upon *your own* sinfulness and weakness. Instead of being so ready to behold the sliver in your brother's eye, consider the plank in your own. (4) Shun the company of talebearers and tattlers; idle gossip is injurious to the soul. (5) If others slander you, see to it that you have a conscience void of offense toward God and man, and then it matters not what others think or say about you.

THE TENTH COMMANDMENT

"Thou shalt not covet thy neighbour's house, thou shalt not covet thy neighbour's wife, nor his manservant, nor his maidservant, nor his ox, nor his ass, nor anything that is thy neighbour's" (Ex. 20:17). That which is here prohibited is concupiscence or an unlawful lusting after what is another man's. In our exposition of the previous Commandments we have pointed out that while their actual terms are confined to the forbidding of outward acts, yet the scope of each one takes in and reaches to the condemnation of everything which has any tendency or occasion to lead to the overt crime. Here in the final precept of the Decalogue we find clear confirmation of the same, for in it God expressly imposes a law upon our spirits, forbidding us to so much as lust after whatever He has forbidden us to perpetrate. The best way to keep men from committing sin in act is to keep them from desiring it in heart. Thus while the authority of each of the first nine Commandments reaches to the mind and the most secret intents of the soul, yet the Lord saw fit to plainly and literally state this in the tenth, where He specifically reprehends the first motions of our hearts toward any object He has fenced, and therefore it is the bond which strengthens the whole.

Evil concupiscence consists of those secret and internal sins that go before the consent of the will and that are the seeds of all evil. Concupiscence or lusting is the firstborn of indwelling depravity, the first risings and expressions of our corrupt nature. It is a violent propensity and inclination toward what is evil, toward that which is contrary to the holy will and command of God. The soul of man is an operative and vigorous creature, ever putting forth activities suitable to its nature. Before the Fall, the soul of man was drawn forth to God as its supreme Object and the End of all its exercise, but when man apostatized and turned from God as his only Good or satisfying Portion, his soul became enamored with the creature. Thus the soul of fallen man, being destitute of Divine grace and spiritual life, craves sinful objects to the slighting of God, and inordinately lusts after things which in themselves are harmless, but become evil because he neither receives them as from God nor uses them for His glory. Concupiscence, then, is that irregular disposition of soul that is here termed "covetousness."

The Puritan Ezekiel Hopkins (to whom we are indebted for much in this chapter, as also for many helpful points in the preceding ones) has pointed out that there are *four* degrees of this sinful concupiscence or coveting. There is the first film or shadow of an evil thought, the imperfect embryo of a sin before it is shaped in us or has any lineaments or features. This is what the Scripture refers to as "every imagination of the thoughts" of the human heart. Such imaginations are expressly declared to be "evil" (Gen. 6:5). Such are the first risings of our corrupt nature toward those sins which are pleasing to our sensual inclinations. They are to be steadfastly watched, hated, and resisted. They are to be stamped upon as the sparks of a dangerous fire, for as soon as they begin to stir within us they pollute our souls. Just as the breathing upon a mirror sullies it, leaving a dimness there, so the very first breathings of an evil desire or thought within one's breast defile the soul.

A further degree of this concupiscence is reached when these evil motions of our corrupt nature are *entertained* in the mind with some degree of complacency. When a sinful object presents itself before a carnal heart there is an inward response that affects that heart with delight and begets a sympathy between it and the object. As in an instance of natural sympathy a man is often pleased with an object before he knows the reason *why* he is, so in an instance of sinful sympathy or response the heart is taken with the object before it has time to consider what there is in that object which so moves and affects it. At the very first sight of a person we many times find that we are more drawn to him than to a whole crowd of others, though all may be equally unknown to us. So the very first glimpse of a sinful thought in our minds reveals that there is that in us which works a regard for the same before we have leisure to examine why it is so. This second form or degree of concupiscence is harder to eject than the former.

If such evil motions are entertained by us, then an *assent* and an approbation to sin follow in one's practical judgment, which, being blinded and carried away by the strength of corrupt and carnal affections, commends the sin to the executive faculty. The understanding is the trier of every deliberate action so that nothing passes into action which has not first passed trial there. Whether this or that action is to be done is the great question canvassed in this court, and all the faculties of the soul await what definite sentence will be here pronounced and thus carried out. Normally two witnesses appear and put in their plea to the understanding or judgment about sin: God's Law and God's vicegerent the conscience. The Law condemns and the conscience cites the Law. But then the affections step in and bribe the judge with promises of pleasure or profit, thereby corrupting the judgment to give its vote and assent to sin. Note how all of this receives illustration in the colloquy between Eve and the Serpent before she partook of the forbidden fruit.

When any sinful motion has thus secured an allowance from the judgment, then it betakes itself to the will for a decree. The understanding having approved it, the will must now resolve to commit it; and then the sin is fully formed within and lacks nothing but opportunity to bring it forth into open action. "But every man is tempted when he is drawn away of his own lust, and enticed; then when lust hath conceived, it bringeth forth (open) sin; and sin, when it is finished, bringeth forth death" (James 1:14, 15). Thus we have endeavored to show what concupiscence or coveting is, and the several degrees of it: the first bubblings up of evil thoughts in our hearts; our delighting in the same (and it is altogether against corrupt nature not to love these firstborn of our own souls); the assent and allowance of our judgment; and the resolution of our wills. Each of these is expressly forbidden by the tenth commandment. And if the sin proceeds any further, then it exceeds the bounds of this commandment and falls under the prohibition of some of the former ones, which more specifically forbid the outward acts of sin.

This final precept, then, utters its solemn protest against sin in the inner life. Herein we may behold and adore the boundless dominion or sovereignty of the great God. He proclaims His rights over the hidden realm of desires. His authority reaches to the soul and conscience and lays an obligation upon our very thoughts and imaginations, which no human laws can do. It would be vain for men to impose statutes upon that of which they can take no cognizance, and therefore our desires and lustings are free from their censure, except so far as they discover themselves by overt acts. But though they escape the commands and notice of men, yet they escape not the scrutiny and sentence of God, for He sees not as men see, neither judges He as men judge. The secrets of all hearts are open and naked before His eyes; not the least breath of a desire can stir in our souls but it is more distinctly visible to Him than the shining of the midday sun is to us.

God's Law, like His knowledge, reaches into the most secret recesses of your soul, searches every corner of your heart, judges those lusts which no human eye can espy, and if they be harbored and approved of, condemns you as a guilty transgressor and worthy of eternal death, no matter how pleasing your external deportment may be. Then how vain it is for us to content ourselves with an *outward* conformity to God's Law! How we should labor to approve *our hearts* in sincerity and purity before God; otherwise we are but pharisaical hypocrites who wash merely the outside of the cup while within we are still full of unclean lusts. How many there are who suppose that God's Law reaches only to the outward man, and that, though they entertain and cherish wicked desires and evil purposes in their hearts, so long as these lusts break not forth into external crimes they will not be charged to their account. But the Day of Judgment will show it is far otherwise. How very few reflect upon heart sins! How very few pray, "Cleanse Thou me from secret faults"! Be not deceived, God is not mocked, and He cannot be duped by external shows.

See here the wisdom of God in setting this commandment at the close of the Decalogue, for it is a fence and guard to all the rest. It is from *inward* defilements of the soul that all our visible sins of word and deed have their rise. All Sabbath-breaking proceeds from the restlessness which is born of unholy desire. "Out of the heart proceed evil thoughts, murders, adulteries" etc. (Matt. 15:19). Observe well that Christ places "evil thoughts" in the front, as the leader of this vile regiment! "Thou shalt not covet." Thou shalt not set thine heart upon, or have the least hankering after, what belongs to another. An objector may say, "It is impossible to prevent the desire for what we admire." Very true, yet in that fact is revealed the fallen condition of man and the desperate wickedness of his heart. That such desire is *sinful and damning* is only discovered in the light of this commandment. He who honestly faces this final precept in the Decalogue must be convicted of his sinfulness and brought to realize his helplessness, or this is its ultimate design. God has given His Holy Law to us in order that we might see the utter *hopelessness* of our case if we are left to ourselves. This He has done in order to shut us up to Christ and the magnitude of His grace toward repentant sinners who will believe on His beloved Son, Who perfectly obeyed the Law and in Whom the Father is well pleased!

A WORD TO PARENTS

One of the saddest and most tragic features of our twentieth-century "Civilization" is the awful prevalence of disobedience on the part of children to their parents during the days of childhood, and their lack of reverence and respect when they grow up. This is evidenced in many ways, and is general, alas, even in the families of professing Christians. In his extensive travels during the past thirty years the writer has sojourned in a great many homes. The piety and beauty of some of them remain as sacred and fragrant memories, but others of them have left the most painful impressions. Children who are self-willed or spoiled, not only bring themselves into perpetual unhappiness but also inflict discomfort upon all who come into contact with them, and auger, by their conduct, evil things for the days to come.

In the vast majority of cases the children are not nearly so much to be blamed as the parents. Failure to honor father and mother, wherever it is found, is in large measure due to parental departure from the Scriptural pattern. Nowadays the father thinks that he has fulfilled his obligations by providing food and raiment for his children, and by acting occasionally as a kind of moral policeman. Too often the mother is content to be a domestic drudge, making herself the slave of her children instead of training them to be useful. She performs many a task which her daughters should do in order to allow them freedom for the frivolities of a giddy set. The consequence has been that the home, which ought to be—for its orderliness, its sanctity, and its reign of love—a miniature heaven on earth, has degenerated into "a filling station for the day and a parking place for the night," as someone has tersely expressed it.

Before outlining the duties of parents toward their children, let it be pointed out that they cannot properly discipline their children unless they have first learned to govern themselves. How can they expect to subdue self-will in their little ones and check the rise of an angry temper if their own passions are allowed free reign? The character of parents is to a very large degree reproduced in their offspring: "And Adam lived a hundred and thirty years and begat a son in his own likeness, after his image" (Gen. 5:3). The parent must himself or herself be in subjection to God if he would lawfully expect obedience from his little ones. This principle is enforced in Scripture again and again: "Thou therefore which teachest another, teachest thou not thyself?" (Rom. 2:20). Of the bishop, that is, elder or pastor, it is written that he must be "one that ruleth well his own house, having his children in subjection with all gravity. For if a man know not how to rule his own house, how shall he take care of the church of God?" (I Tim. 3:5, 6). And if a man or woman knows not how to rule his own spirit (Prov. 25:28), how shall he care for his offspring.

God has entrusted to parents a most solemn charge, and yet a most precious privilege. It is not too much to say that in their hands are deposited the hope and blessing, or else the curse and plague, of the next generation. Their families are the nurseries of both Church and State, and according to the cultivating of them now will be their fruitfulness hereafter. Oh, how prayerfully and carefully should you who are parents discharge your trust. Most assuredly God will require an account of the children from your hands, for they are His, and only lent to your care and keeping. The task assigned you is no easy one, especially in these superlatively evil days. Nevertheless, if trustfully and earnestly sought, the grace of God will be found sufficient in this responsibility as in others. The Scriptures supply us with rules to go by, with promises to lay hold of, and, we may add, with fearful warnings lest we treat the matter lightly.

Instruct Your Children

We have space to mention but four of the principal duties devolving on parents. First, it is your duty to instruct your children. "And these words which I command thee this day, shall be in thine heart: and thou shalt teach them diligently unto thy children, and shalt talk of them when thou sittest in thine house, and when thou walkest by the way, and when thou liest down, and when thou risest up" (Deut. 6:6, 7). This work is far too important to allocate to others; parents, and not Sabbath School teachers, are Divinely required to educate their little ones. Nor is this to be an occasional or sporadic thing, but one that is to have constant attention. The glorious character of God, the requirements of His holy Law, the exceeding sinfulness of sin, the wondrous gift of His Son, and the fearful doom which is the certain portion of all who despise and reject Him are to be brought repeatedly before the minds of your little ones. "They are too young to understand such things" is the Devil's argument to deter you from discharging your duty.

"And ye fathers, provoke not your children to wrath: but bring them up in the nurture and admonition of the Lord" (Eph. 6:4). It is to be noted that the "fathers" are here specifically addressed, and this for two reasons: (1) because they are the heads of their families and their government is especially committed to them; and (2) because they are prone to transfer this duty to their wives. This instruction is to be given by reading to them the Holy Scriptures and enlarging upon those things most agreeable to their age. This should be followed by catechizing them. A continued discourse to the young is not nearly so effective as when it is diversified by questions and answers. If they know they will be questioned on what you read, they will listen more closely, and the formulating of answers teaches them to think for themselves. Such a method is also found to make the memory more retentive, for answering definite questions fixes more specific ideas in the mind. Observe how often Christ asked His disciples questions.

Be a Good Example

Second, good instruction is to be accompanied by good example. That teaching which issues only from the lips is not at all likely to sink any deeper than the ears. Children are particularly quick to detect inconsistencies and to despise hypocrisy. It is at this point that parents need to be most on their faces before God, daily seeking from Him that grace that they so sorely need and that He alone can supply. What care you need to take, lest you say or do anything before your children that would tend to corrupt their minds or be of evil consequence for them to follow! How you need to be constantly on your guard against anything which might render you mean and contemptible in the eyes of those who should respect and revere you! The parent is not only to instruct his children in the ways of holiness, but is himself to *walk* before them in those ways, and show by his practice and demeanor what a pleasant and profitable thing it is to be regulated by the Divine Law.

In a Christian home the supreme aim should be household piety—the honoring of God at all times. Everything else must be subordinated to this high purpose. In the matter of family life, neither husband nor wife can throw on the other all the responsibility for the religious character of the home. The mother is most certainly required to supplement the efforts of the father, for the children enjoy far more of her company than they do of his. If there is a tendency in fathers to be too strict and severe, mothers are prone to be too lax and lenient; and they need to be much on their guard against anything which would weaken their husband's authority. When he has forbidden a thing, she must not give her consent to it. It is striking to note that the exhortation of Ephesians 6:4 is preceded by instruction to "be filled with the Spirit" (5:18), while the parallel exhortation in Colossians 3:21 is preceded by the exhortation to "let the Word of Christ dwell in you richly" (v. 16), showing that parents cannot possibly discharge their duties unless they are filled with the Spirit and the Word.

Discipline Your Children

Third, instruction and example is to be enforced by correction and discipline. This means, first of all, the exercise of authority—the proper reign of Law. Of "the father of the faithful" God said, "For I know him, that he will command his children and his household after him, and they shall keep the way of the Lord to do justice and judgment; that the Lord may bring upon Abraham that which He hath spoken of him" (Gen. 18:19). Ponder this carefully, Christian fathers. Abraham did more than proffer good advice; he enforced law and order in his household. The rules he administered had for their design the keeping of "the way of the Lord"—that which was right in His sight. And this duty was performed by the patriarch in order that the blessing of God might rest on his family. No family can be properly brought up without household laws, which include reward and punishment, and these are especially important in early childhood, when as yet moral character is unformed and moral motives are not understood or appreciated.

Rules should be simple, clear, reasonable, and inflexible like the Ten Commandments—a few great moral rules, instead of a multitude of petty restrictions. One way of needlessly provoking children to wrath is to hamper them with a thousand trifling restrictions and minute regulations that are capricious and are due to a fastidious temper in the parent. It is of vital importance for the child's future good that he or she should be brought into subjection at an early age. An untrained child means a lawless adult. Our prisons are crowded with those who were allowed to have their own way during their minority. The least offense of a child against the rulers of the home ought not to pass without due correction, for if he finds leniency in one direction or toward one offense he will expect the same toward others. And then disobedience will become more frequent till the parent has no control save that of brute force.

The teaching of Scripture is crystal clear on this point. "Foolishness is bound in the heart of a child; but the rod of correction shall drive it far from him" (Prov. 22:15; and cf. 23:13, 14). Therefore God has said, "He that spareth the rod hateth his son: but he that loveth him chasteneth him betimes (speedily)" (Prov. 13:24). And again, "Chasten thy son while there is hope, and let not thy soul spare for his crying" (Prov. 19:18). Let not a foolish fondness stay thee. Certainly God loves His children with a much deeper parental affection that you can love yours, yet He tells us, "As many as I love, I rebuke and chasten" (Rev. 3:19; and cf. Heb. 12:6). "The rod and reproof give wisdom: but a child left to himself bringeth his mother to shame" (Prov. 29:15). Such severity must be used in his early years, before age and obstinacy have hardened the child against the fear and smart of correction. Spare the rod, and you spoil the child; use it not on him, and you lay up one for your own back.

It should hardly need pointing out that the above Scriptures are by no means teaching that a reign of terror is to mark the home life. Children can be governed and chastened in such a way that they lose not their respect and affection for their parents. Beware of souring their temper by unreasonable demands, or provoking their wrath by striking them to vent your own rage. The parent is to punish a disobedient child not because he is angry, but because it is right—because God requires it, and the welfare of the child demands it. Never make a threat which you have no intention of executing, nor a promise you do not mean to perform. Remember that for your children to be well informed is good, but for them to be well controlled is better.

Pay close attention to the unconscious influences of a child's surroundings. Study how to make your home attractive, not by introducing carnal and worldly things, but by noble ideals, by the inculcating of a spirit of unselfishness, by genial and happy fellowship. Separate the little ones from evil associates. Watch carefully the periodicals and books which come into your home, the occasional guests which sit at your table, and the companionships that your children form. Parents often carelessly let others have free access to their children who undermine the parental authority, overturn the parental ideals, and sow seeds of frivolity and iniquity before they are aware. Never let your child spend a night among strangers. So train your children that your girls will be useful and helpful members of their generation and your boys industrious and self-supporting.

Pray for Your Children

Fourth, the last and most important duty, respecting both the temporal and spiritual good of your children, is fervent supplication to God for them; for without this all the rest will be ineffectual. Means are unavailing unless the Lord blesses them. The Throne of Grace is to be earnestly implored that your efforts to bring up your children for God may be crowned with success. True, there must be a humble submission to His sovereign will, a bowing before the truth of Election. On the other hand, it is the privilege of faith to lay hold of the Divine promises and to remember that the effectual fervent prayer of a righteous man availeth much. Of holy Job it is recorded concerning his sons and daughters that he "rose up early in the morning and offered burnt offerings according to the number of them all" (Job 1:5). A prayerful atmosphere should pervade the home and be breathed by all who share it.

(The above chapter, "A Word to Parents," can be obtained in tract form from Chapel Library, Box 1335, Venice, Florida 33595.)

INDEX OF SCRIPTURES QUOTED